Your Complete Forecast 2018 Horoscope

CANCER

Your Complete Forecast 2018 Horoscope

CANCER

BEJAN DARUWALLA
With
NASTUR DARUWALLA

Ranvir Books
HARPER element

First published in India in 2017 by Harper Element
An imprint of HarperCollins *Publishers*

P-ISBN: 978-93-5277-336-7
E-ISBN: 978-93-5277-337-4

2 4 6 8 10 9 7 5 3 1

HarperCollins *Publishers*
A-75, Sector 57, Noida, Uttar Pradesh 201301, India
1 London Bridge Street, London, SE1 9GF, United Kingdom
2 Bloor Street East, Toronto, Ontario M4W 1A8, Canada
Lvl 13, 201 Elizabeth Street (PO Box A565, NSW, 1235), Sydney NSW 2000, Australia
195 Broadway, New York, NY 10007, USA

Typeset in 11.5/15 Sabon
By Saanvi Graphics, Noida

Printed and bound at
MicroPrints (India), New Delhi

Contents

CANCER

23 June–22 July

'It is hard to imagine what the world would be like without the geometry of Euclid, the philosophy of Pythagoras, the logic and literature of Aristotle and the fables of Aesop, not forgetting the Olympic games with their spirit of peace and brotherhood. Words such as philanthropy, harmony, music, architecture and ecology that we use so often today are derived from Greek.'

I am very sure that the above paragraph has motivated and inspired you. You Cancerians are intuitive and psychic; therefore you must have felt in your bones and marrow that the goodies of life are coming your way.

- **Element:** Water

- **Ruling planet:** Moon
- **Colours:** White, opal, iridescent silvery hues, smoky grey, sea green and blue
- **Colours that promote love, romance, and social harmony:** Black, indigo
- **Colours that promote earning power:** Gold, orange.
- **Gems:** Moonstone, pearl
- **Metal:** Silver
- **Scents:** Jasmine, sandalwood
- **Quality:** Cardinal (=activity)
- **Quality most needed for balance:** Mood control
- **Strongest virtues:** Emotional sensitivity, tenacity, the urge to nurture

- **Deepest need:** A harmonious home and family life
- **Characteristics to avoid:** Oversensitivity, negative moods
- **Best day of the week:** Monday
- **Body parts ruled by Cancer:** The breasts and stomach. Cancerians love to eat and have to fight obesity in later years, and also digestive ailments.
- **Cities:** Amsterdam, New York, Istanbul, Tokyo, Algiers
- **Countries:** Scotland, Holland, New Zealand and Paraguay
- **Number:** Two
- **Flowers:** White lily, acanthus, white rose, larkspur, convolvulus, water lily, all white flowers

- **Trees:** All trees, particularly those rich in sap
- **Foods:** Milk, fish, fruits and vegetables with a high water content, white and red cabbage, and herbs such as verbena and tarragon are all linked with Cancer

SPECIAL MESSAGE FROM BEJAN AND NASTUR

Emotionally, Cancerians act and react in the same way the crab moves: sideways. They avoid confrontations and usually aren't comfortable in discussing what they feel. Cancers are intuitive and sometimes psychic. Experience flows through them emotionally. They are often moody and always changeable; their interests and social circles shift constantly. Once a Cancer trusts you, however, he lets you in on his most private world. Summary: Romance and finance fuse happily for you. Health safeguards will be essential. Plenty of movement physically, mentally, emotionally, spiritually, points out Ganesha, and His is the last word.

JUPITER

'Whatever defect I have of eye, of heart, of mind, or whatever exam there is, may Brihaspati (Jupiter) remedy it. Gracious to us he, the Lord of the world' – Yajur Veda 36:2. Yes, Jupiter in Indian astrology is best known as the 'Lord of the world'. And Jupiter will be in your fifth angle from 10 October 2017 to 8 November 2018.

By Western Astrology, Jupiter has a very great influence on the sign of Cancer. It spells prosperity. When Jupiter is in the fifth angle (or the sign Cancer), it is even more powerful and beneficial. In 2018, Jupiter will be in the fifth angle.

Jupiter will unfold for you the following: Your heart will sing, '*I drink to myself and one another/And may that one another be she!*', even if you are a teetotaller. Rightly so too. Jupiter will make you attractive and charming and thus draw in your opposite number.

Also, 2018 is for journeys, long-distance connections, socializing, friendship and fraternity. Yes, you will be working like a Trojan and savouring life to the maximum.

Let me begin by saying that this year will be significant for good health, confidence, prestige, status, recognition, rewards, new opportunities, travel, intuition, philosophy, spirituality and wisdom. Need more be said? Jupiter will lubricate your intellect, pep it up with all sorts of pills and goodies so to say, and will galvanize you into great action!

Love, romance, hobbies, children (starting of conception, or actual delivery of a child); exceptional creative pursuits requiring imagination and organization; the use of tantra and mantra; a possible recall of your past life or lives (you are most welcome to have your own opinion of past life or reincarnation); success in property affairs, buying and selling or just developing; new and vast outlets of entertainment and amusement, or it could be a different way or style of entertainment (example a film story, a terrific directional venture); speculation and indulgence in games of chance (example horse racing) are foretold. A word of warning, please. This is only a solar-scopic reading, not a real horoscopic one. Results and predictions are therefore not guaranteed to come correct.

SATURN

By Western astrology, Saturn will be in your seventh angle from 21 December 2017 to 22 March 2020. Let me say straight away that Saturn will blow hot and cold for you. The biggest advantage of it is that you will never have a dull moment in your life. It will be up and down and roundabout. It will be like a merry-go-round. Be sure of changes in personal and professional relationships. That is the real secret and clue to the purpose of Saturn in your seventh angle. The other noteworthy features are:

a) Connections, contacts, reaching out to people and places;
b) Journey, ceremony, legal matters;
c) Public relationships and competition, change of locale/surrounding;
d) Collaborations and cooperation.

Ganesha dances full of jest, humour and slight mischief. In 2018, Saturn will be in a fine placing with Jupiter. Therefore, if changes are forced upon you take it in the right spirit. I know you are very sensitive, very kind, very loving, and therefore you get hurt very easily. Ganesha and Allah say, accept changes naturally and then move forward in your life. Prayers, meditations, mantras, tolerance, understanding the other person's point of view will most certainly help. If you like, you may recite the mantra, 'Shree Ram, Jay Ram, Jay Jay Ram'. Take care of lawsuits and quarrels or very petty matters. The surprising part of it all is that attainment of status and recovery of lost wealth are also very possible.

Please take 2018 and 2019 as one unit because Saturn will be in your seventh angle throughout.

MARS

Moon is the main planet for you Cancerians. But Moon changes signs every ¼ day. Therefore, I am taking the next important planet Mars for you. Mars will help you in diametrically opposite directions, namely, a) romance, hobbies, children, creative pursuits, games of chance and b) prestige, profession, work areas, promotion, profit, success. Especially important periods for it will be 1 to 20 January, 13 August to 10 September and 16 November to 31 December 2018. July, your birth month, will show the way to happiness and health.

URANUS

Uranus will be responsible for changes in the nature and scope of your work. Even if you are ninety years old, your brain cells will jiggle and jump and you will be able to work efficiently. Evidently this should make you feel very confident. As you all know, confidence is certainly the sister, if not the mother, of success. Finally, I say very sincerely and humbly, 'May Ganga Maiya go with you emotional, sensitive, kind, nervous, slightly insecure Cancerians.'

NEPTUNE

Neptune is your best bet. How and why? Neptune will be in your ninth angle of inspiration, imagination, psychic powers, religion, spirituality and perhaps glimpses of God or nature or whatever else you believe in. Secondly, Neptune rules over the sea. The element of you Cancerians is water. Therefore, once again Neptune will give you an insight into the nature of all things above including creation itself. Time to invent, time to discover, time for a bit of romance, time for great fun, time for making merry and if you want you can also marry. Choice is yours. In short, an excellent mix of joy and sorrow awaits you.

PLUTO

Pluto embraces Saturn in your seventh angle. Result? Exciting adventure in all areas of human contacts, attachments and affairs. It means you will be lively and possibly dancing on your toes with joy and sorrow both. Let me now make a confession. I am also a Cancerian and this will probably apply to me. Journeys and ceremonies are very probable. My advice to you once again is, let life take its own force and go with the flow. Your circle of friends will increase and therefore your orbit of influence will be as wide as the sky itself.

MONTHLY ROUND-UP

January: Power, pelf, perks, promotion, prosperity;

February: Finances and family;

March: Contacts and joy;

April: Property, parents, renovation/ decoration, parents, in-laws;

May: Joy, creativity, children, hobbies, you make news and win others over;

June: Work, funds, employment, health and medical check-up, servants, subordinates;

July: Marriage, ties, love, collaborations, romance, meeting and reaching out to people and places;

August: Health, funds, vitality, tantra and mantra, change of locale, moving;

September: Journeys, publicity, ceremonies, collaborations, functions, rites and religion;

October: Stepping up on efficiency, work, status, prestige, taking care of parents, elders;

November: Help, socializing, friendship, fraternity, camaraderie; **December:**

Expenses, losses, spirituality, helping others, charity, long-distance connections.

HAPPINESS QUOTA: 83 per cent

WEEKLY REVIEW (BY PHASES OF THE MOON)

2 JANUARY: FULL MOON IN CANCER

You start the year in a true sunburst of glory – you have the Midas touch in all you undertake, all you do! Home and domestic issues are quiet and composed but work will be wonderfully rewarding and satisfying. It is the money angle, though that spells out rewards, satisfaction, success. Bonds, securities, joint finance, perhaps even golden handshakes, as you move on to something different, something better.

8 JANUARY: LAST QUARTER IN LIBRA

True creativity, intellectual genius, even brilliance, joy and success in relationships. What a trend! You have all the right skills as well as the right ideas. Glamour, inspiration, chutzpah give you achievements and success in all your undertakings and with the people who matter most to you. And here I'm talking of the entirely personal relationships and bonds that make it all worthwhile!

17 JANUARY: NEW MOON IN CAPRICORN

From the very first few days of the year, the going has been good, as I've pointed out. It is especially good now in terms of both personal and professional growth, progress, recognition. Both better health and better money make you much more dynamic. This will reflect on not only your work angle – that much is obvious – but on the quality and tone of your relationships, your interaction with people in general and with your special people.

24 JANUARY: FIRST QUARTER IN TAURUS

More and more is what Ganesha has decided to give you. He seems to be showing us what true generosity is all about. There is good health, marvellous romance, joy in relationships, falling in love all over again. Some diehard romantics like me, in fact, never fall out of it. It's good to be in love with life – keeps one young at heart! Position and status, power, prestige, recognition all register tremendous gains too.

31 JANUARY: FULL MOON IN LEO

The year 2018 started very well for you and has continued to be good. Anyone might be justified in thinking it won't last, but it does! You get more good things and they are the type to last. There is a renewal of faith, an avowal of spiritual leanings, prayer, reverence for the Supreme Being. Even the philosophical, the metaphysical, the life one leads (?) after death, will exercise and brighten your mind.

7 FEBRUARY: LAST QUARTER IN SCORPIO

Two trends for this month instead of one predominant theme. On the one hand, you will seek solitude to promote meditation, contemplation, your inner health. This will be the direct offshoot of last week's spirituality. On the other hand, you relate so well to people, and are so energetic, confident, successful that the angle of entertainment, hospitality, social intercourse will be equally energized.

15 FEBRUARY: NEW MOON IN AQUARIUS

You will be closer than ever to your family, your loved ones and above all, to your own self, your identity, your individuality. Your heritage and ancestry, your roots will be more important than ever. You'll seek to fix them more firmly in your own consciousness and awareness. All this will happen despite a good deal of travel. It could, of course, even be because of it.

23 FEBRUARY: FIRST QUARTER IN GEMINI

Dreams are coming true – with the full moon phase in your own sign. Long-cherished hopes, ambitions, wishes will now become concrete realities. A sense of achievement is a fine way to feel. Ganesha gives it to you now, but he adds on a warning against pushing too hard and expecting too much from others.

2 MARCH: FULL MOON IN VIRGO

You are not workaholic the way you can often be. But they have great focus, determination, single-mindedness. In this phase, it is these qualities that will direct you to the work arena. Please note the word 'arena' – where gladiators went out to win in combats to the thunderous applause of spectators. You will also attach problems, disputes, perhaps even some of them pertaining to family property.

9 MARCH: LAST QUARTER IN SAGITTARIUS

You will be brilliant and successful – impressively so – in your professional life/career/job. Politicians would kill to have the kind of dream run you've been having since the start of 2018. And Ganesha tells me that it will continue for some months more. All this, as I've said earlier, reflects gloriously and beautifully on your family life, on your love/marriage interactions, on your dealings with both parents and children.

17 MARCH: NEW MOON IN PISCES

You feel that you must give your best, perhaps your all to the family you hold so dear. Particularly so for your spouse/partner/lover, with whom there are joys, the perennial delights that come from the union of both flesh and soul. This is not an exaggeration – I'm just trying to describe how good it will all be!

24 MARCH: FIRST QUARTER IN CANCER

Marvellous but hectic activity now. It's so good that you wouldn't have it any other way. And the activity will centre around money and honey (love) – my favourite phrase. Both will be brilliantly satisfying and you'll be thinking of all possible ways to keep it that way. You're on to so many good things that only a fool would let them go. And a fool you're not.

31 MARCH: FULL MOON IN LIBRA

Recreation, wining and dining, being entertained, extending hospitality – having a rare good old time is what I see you doing now. Joy that is boundless and deep comes to you in the love/ marriage angle. There could be both love and marriage happening now too. Sometimes love preoccupies a person so that friendship gets excluded.

8 APRIL: LAST QUARTER IN CAPRICORN

You may not want to, but you'll still have to focus very strongly on the finances now. You have to make some bold moves and decisions, the right choices according to your own conviction of where money and security lie. It won't be a time for boldness, though, on the family scene. There could be disputes and problems to sort out, feelings of real or imagined neglect to soothe, some gestures of conciliation to be made.

16 APRIL: NEW MOON IN ARIES

You will consciously slow down the pace at which you're living and make an effort to take things easy. Maybe the allegations of neglect have rankled, even if they are not true. In fact, I should have said 'specially if they're not true'. You bring a sense of style and lots of flair to your handling of people you're close to, sparing no effort. Even though it's done with restraint, there's no holding back.

22 APRIL: FIRST QUARTER IN LEO

Now that your personal equations are ticking over so smoothly – to the mutual satisfaction of all concerned, I must add – your public persona has to live up to the gloss and glamour. Let me assure you that it does. You are gracious, warm, humane, yet so brilliant and impressive that people are flooded by it!

30 APRIL: FULL MOON IN SCORPIO

No one can ever be in doubt of the fact that your approach to work is so committed that it's almost perfect! Your work angle is in focus now, and the results of your own willing, determined efforts. Your publicity will be so good that you might not believe in it. You will be genuinely helpful, sharing, sincere with your co-workers and colleagues, efficient with bosses, humane and fair with employees.

8 MAY: LAST QUARTER IN AQUARIUS

Your expenses will be something else – they're so high. You've spent generously on all fronts; in fact, money was burning a hole in your pockets. Now you have the money to make sure that you don't let anyone down, or renege on promises, deals, payments. If you have the income to cope – and you do; Ganesha ensures it – you're willing to spend some more.

15 MAY: NEW MOON IN TAURUS

You will be relaxed, comfortable, at ease, easy-going. All this is especially good considering that you're now hobnobbing with the rich and famous, rubbing shoulders with the top brass, with people of distinction. You have the confidence to hold your own. It also makes it easier to continue with your devotion to family and loved ones, to older people and to those who depend on you.

22 MAY: FIRST QUARTER IN VIRGO

Skill, efficiency, single-minded concentration and of course, efficiency – these are what you get now. They're all directed to your work at which you're truly brilliant without being self-centred. It is another matter entirely that you are equally brilliant at fun, socializing, pleasurable activities.

29 MAY: FULL MOON IN SAGITTARIUS

Something will transpire to make you take a very different line, a new modus operandi. It will be a mental shift, not an action that makes you withdraw. What is hidden, mysterious, unrevealed will appeal to you. Parapsychology, metaphysics, little-known sciences, exploration and archaeology, exploration of the mind, of genes, of cosmic truths.

6 JUNE: LAST QUARTER IN PISCES

If you are analytical, look back on the success and glory of the past period, you will feel thankful of course, but will also seek to analyse, search for reasons for it. You will realize now that you get your power, strength, motives – all of them – from your joy in family, domesticity, the bonds of matrimony, love, kinship.

13 JUNE: NEW MOON IN GEMINI

Power: one word sums up the heightened awareness and activity of this phase in your own sign. Many benefits are in store for you now. You may have a wish-fulfilment, the realization of a dream. Relationships and ties, bonds and tie-ups are what matter most from the personal bonds of love and matrimony to the professional partnerships, collaborations that lead to future gain.

20 JUNE: FIRST QUARTER IN VIRGO

All the power plays of the last period will show some really fast, and really glorious results. Rewards, recognition, all the parameters of success are yours once more. When I say all, I mean all. More money, more perks, more benefits add up to a fine financial angle too.

28 JUNE: FULL MOON IN CAPRICORN

If your dreams didn't come true – or not quite the way you had envisaged – in your moon quarter, they might be clicking now. Or there could be other dreams, wishes, ambitions that take concrete shape now. Whichever way you look at it, the realization of hopes and plans should be happening now, unless there's something in your personal horoscope that makes it otherwise.

6 JULY: LAST QUARTER IN ARIES

True creativity – and all the fields that hinge on that, like media, infotech, the arts and literature, in particular, event and portfolio management; a vast range indeed – will be greatly favoured. People will respond to your charm and charisma, relationships will be revitalized. So also, will love. However, what is most vital, most alive is your intensely personal, private space where not even love/spouse can enter.

13 JULY: NEW MOON IN CANCER

You may find all of a sudden that there is a dynamic, diametric shift from the trends of the last period. The home, the domestic scene, will take up most of your time and attention. It's not that you won't work; it's also not that you won't play. But both work and pleasure will be coloured and influenced by family involvements.

19 JULY: FIRST QUARTER IN LIBRA

You will realize that life in the fast lane is over for the time being. It's not that you're suddenly taking a break/holiday and leading a relaxed, easy-going life. There will be intense but internalized activity as you lay bare your soul, your innermost being, before your own eyes. Go in for some intensive, deep introspection, try to determine your values and future course of action.

27 JULY: FULL MOON IN AQUARIUS

You have decided that your family is your first priority, and this entire period is a confirmation of that belief, that conviction. In family are included siblings, cousins, older relatives, parents, in-laws. Even the fair amount of travel you engage in helps renew old ties, acquaintances, contacts. Your personal sense of worth and self-esteem will be very important in this context.

AUGUST 4: LAST QUARTER IN TAURUS

You may look back on the last period as a small interlude of peace in your hectic, schedule. All the activities that you were putting off are now back with a bang, and you're off at the same pace. You will be involved with lots of dedicated hard work, determined effort and equally deep emotional commitment, intense and vibrant love and passion and even deep sexual bondage.

11 AUGUST: NEW MOON IN LEO

You will shine as perhaps the brightest star in the social firmament, entertaining hospitably and lavishly, being a welcome guest, partying and socializing. All this will be done with your usual panache, but perhaps this is a facade, a mask you're wearing to cover up what I spoke of in the last period. That is a deeply personal side of you that you may not want others to see.

18 AUGUST: FIRST QUARTER IN SCORPIO

You will be quiet, introspective, thinking of lifestyle changes, the quieter life, more placid ways and your own inner values. You realize that there must be deep-rooted and fundamental changes and are both willing and keen to make them. It's not just boredom or ennui that makes you think this way. It is a firm belief – and you wish to act on it.

26 AUGUST: FULL MOON IN PISCES

You may wish to withdraw from the world, but it's a moot point whether the world will let you! Not this period, at any rate, no matter how keen your desire to do so. Communication – in every possible manner, by every possible means – would sum up your activities in this period. You're brilliant as a negotiator/troubleshooter and take some wise decisions to defuse tensions too.

3 SEPTEMBER: LAST QUARTER IN GEMINI

All the zodiac signs get activated, even stirred up, during moon phases in their own sign. It is not noticeable in the new moon phase, because that is when a trend starts for the lunar month. Achievements and gains of all kinds come to you now, as do greater efficiency, skills and expertise. It is not, says Ganesha, the time for complacency and overconfidence even if you have so much going for you.

9 SEPTEMBER: NEW MOON IN VIRGO

A fine sense of direction and focus come to you. You know how to wear the mantle of success and which way to go in the future. In money matters too. Additionally, you are able to accept your role in life and also your responsibilities – to work, to family, and to your own self. Your personal growth and development will be important during this period.

16 SEPTEMBER: FIRST QUARTER IN SAGITTARIUS

Both love and family angles will be pleasant, soothing, peaceful. Children and spouse in particular make for truly contented moments. There is closer bonding and oneness in both love and affection. It makes you calm, well adjusted and at peace with yourself. It also gives you an almost cosmic awareness, a deep faith and spiritual strength.

25 SEPTEMBER: FULL MOON IN ARIES

With the special insights of the last period, you will examine all your relationships almost under a microscope. You will also seek to put them into perspective. You redefine your own role to your parents, your children, your spouse or lover or mate. In all, you will seek to fulfil the expectations they have of you. These expectations will not be voiced by them but perceived by you.

2 OCTOBER: LAST QUARTER IN CANCER

The pressures of work never go away from you. In addition, you will feel the pressures, pulls, demands. It is still a time for success and achievements, though not as spectacular as during the first half of the year. That is the way it was for you last year too. And like last year, this year too, you find that the first half spelt out as material/worldly success and the second half, as spiritual emotional growth.

9 OCTOBER: NEW MOON IN LIBRA

The tensions, worries, fears and anxieties of the past period will fade away now. Ease and comfort in living, peace and calm of mind are experienced. Work/business/career will find you greatly successful. In fact, you have been successful right through but the satisfaction quotient will be much higher now. It is not just experienced professionally.

16 OCTOBER: FIRST QUARTER IN CAPRICORN

Fun, family, entertaining and finance – once again, they are all there, but on a much larger scale now. Therefore, heavier expenses are bound to happen too. Finances too will not mean family or domestic budgeting alone. There could be international transactions and transfers of funds, joint finances, deals abroad, also collaborations mergers, tie-ups.

24 OCTOBER: FULL MOON IN TAURUS

You are in a mood to solve problems, extend help, support commitment. These problems could be global or world-related, or closer to home. Your attitude will be equally sincere and caring towards both. Also, while dealing with financial matters like generating capital, dealing with loans, trusts, endowments, you take equally good care of your dependents, children, servants, in-laws.

31 OCTOBER: LAST QUARTER IN LEO

If Ganesha gave you no spare time. He must be fair and give you the energy, willpower, strength to cope. And that's just what you experience now. Love and money angles will be particularly energized. Health will be better. You'll also take better care of yourself physically. You want to be fighting fit, in appearance and turnout too.

7 NOVEMBER: NEW MOON IN SCORPIO

Realizing that you cannot live in splendid isolation, as you were tempted to do in the previous period, you now brush up communication skills, and public relations. New places will attract you. New friends enthuse and excite you. There is a glorious exchange of ideas, opinions, hopes and plans. Your enthusiasm, energy, joie de vivre – all register wonderful gains!

15 NOVEMBER: FIRST QUARTER IN AQUARIUS

You got so much of social interaction and friendship that you will now raise it to the level of a fine art! This is no exaggeration. New friends and old, and even your rivals, competitors, enemies – you interact with them all. Only the ways will vary! Your performance at interviews, meetings, presentations, debates will be dazzling. And it's not just a performance – you are truly communicating.

23 NOVEMBER: FULL MOON IN GEMINI

People and people and people. That's how important they will be for you. As I said in the last period, even rivals and competitors. You are now confident, full of energy, daring, enterprising, ready to take on everyone. You are loving, warm, caring – and busy. You will be popular, successful, very much in demand at social gatherings, functions, ceremonies.

30 NOVEMBER: LAST QUARTER IN VIRGO

I told you that Ganesha was pleased. Therefore, he gives you many rewards – success, power, recognition and prestige, perks and benefits. These are the tangibles. In addition, his gifts are greater intuition and perceptiveness, therefore much more kindness, tolerance, warmth, sincere caring and affection.

7 DECEMBER: NEW MOON IN SAGITTARIUS

We talked of your spiritual gains just above. It is now that you will find them much more apparent. You will realize just how important true values and idealism have become for you. They form part of your psyche, your ethos. Your desire for excellence and achievement will still be there. Now, however, you strive for personal growth and development, for excellence in the spiritual, moral, social and personal spheres.

15 DECEMBER: FIRST QUARTER IN PISCES

You will not seek to exhibit or show off your personal values, idealism, even convictions. All this is bound to reflect beautifully on both your professional life/work and your personal relationships. Perhaps you are afraid it will all get dissipated or frittered away. Perhaps it is too intensely personal to be displayed. However, you will be concerned about how others see you, about the image you project.

22 DECEMBER: FULL MOON IN CANCER

You will have that desire and the confidence to try to excel in new fields; new challenges will be faced, fresh skills acquired. You are not content to just sit back and congratulate. You want fresh new worlds to conquer. You want to prove yourself all over again – to yourself, and perhaps, to Ganesha. Perhaps you feel that where you're happiest, where things go best for you in terms of satisfaction, is at home.

29 DECEMBER: LAST QUARTER IN LIBRA

You will seek to address disputes, contentions regarding family/joint property; perhaps there could be family funds or even a divorce to be negotiated. What you realize now is that that is where you're needed the most. In spite of this, you are not willing to compromise one iota with your career/professional goals and demands.

Achievements 2018

By the grace of Lord Ganesh, my son Nastur found patrons in Shri Raj Kumar Jatia and his son, Shri Adarsh Jatia, the owners of Four Seasons, Mumbai, and Provenance Four Seasons Private Residences. May patience and hard work take my son to the top of the world where Shri Raj Kumar Jatia stands like a shining star. Nastur was graciously invited by the noble business tycoon, Byram Avari, of Avari Group of Hotels, Karachi, and his wife, Goshpi Avari, to attend their fiftieth wedding anniversary.

I bless prosperity upon Prayush Poddar, his father and his family. May his company, AMP Universal Realty Pvt. Ltd, prosper. He has been like a son to me.

May the grace of Lord Ganesha bless Police Commissioner Anupam Singh Gehlot of Rajkot. He has always stood by my family, in good times and bad. Peace and prosperity prevail in Rajkot because of his sincere efforts.

BJP National vice-president and Rajya Sabha member, Vinay Sahasrabuddhe is a very fine and noble gentleman. He was gracious enough to arrange a meeting with Maharashtra chief minister Devendra Fadnavis, who was dynamic and touched by the divine.

Body Language

Ganesha believed astrology to be all about behaviour, relationships and how to handle them. Therefore, the guidelines given below should help you to understand yourself and others. Any information that adds to the knowledge of oneself is always welcome. Here are some examples of body language and its possible interpretations:

POSITIVE VIBES

- Open arms and hands: open and receptive
- Leaning forward: interested in conversation

- Smiling or attempting to be humorous: friendly
- Eye contact with occasional, natural breaks in the stare: focused and curious
- Nodding while listening: attentive and alert
- Open palms: approachable and trusting
- Gesturing with hands while talking: genuinely involved in the conversation
- Upright shoulders: positivity

NEGATIVE VIBES

- Crossed arms and/or legs: closed off, defensive, reserved or suspicious
- Standing with hands inside the pockets: unsure or suspicious
- Fidgeting, running one's tongue along one's teeth, playing with hair

or jewellery or tapping feet: nervous and/or bored

- Lack of eye contact or staring too intently and unblinkingly: untrustworthy
- Leaning back: uncomfortable
- Clasping hands behind the head while leaning back: seeking power
- Drooping shoulders: unsure

Colours of Life

Ganesha believes that life is like a rainbow. Life is like nature, full of abundance and variety. The best part of it is you can actually experiment with the colours given below and have fun. Here, we combine abundance and a variety of colours for joy, use, experience.

- **Energetic:** Red
- **Sporty:** Red, orange
- **Exuberant:** Orange
- **Active:** Orange, yellow
- **Modern:** Yellow

- **Invigorating:** Green, yellow
- **Sunny:** Green, yellow
- **Fresh:** Green
- **Luminous:** Blue, Green
- **Hypnotic:** Blue
- **Regal:** Blue, violet
- **Exotic:** Violet
- **Playful:** Red, orange, violet, yellow
- **Vibrant:** Green, red

(Your astrologer admits that this colour system is *not* his own.)

Important Dates

I have always believed that the fear of failure has never led to advancement of knowledge. These dates and directions may differ from the various trends and forecasts mentioned elsewhere in the book. A different direction is being pursued here. This is a totally different ball game. This is to be taken as an experiment on a mass scale with the readers themselves as guinea pigs (willingly, I hope).

Please remember, as a rule, your birth month and the seventh month from it (including itself) will be hectic. For example, if your birth month is March, the seventh from it will be September. There will be tremendous franticness in both these months.

January: 1–2, 5–7, 10–12, 15–16, 19–20, 23–24, 28–29

February: 2–3, 7–8, 11–12, 16–17, 20–21, 24–26, 29

March: 1–2, 5–6, 10–11, 14–15, 18–19, 22–24, 27–29

April: 1–3, 6–7, 10–11, 14–16, 19–20, 24–25, 29–30.

May: 3–4, 7–8 12–13, 16–18, 21–23, 26–27, 31

June: 4–5, 8–9 , 12–14, 17–19, 22–24, 27–28

July: 1–2, 5–6, 10–11, 15–16, 20–21, 24–26, 29–30

August: 2–3, 6–7, 11–12,16–17, 21–22, 25–26, 29–30

September: 2–4, 7–9, 12–14, 17–18, 21–11, 25–26, 30

October: 1, 4–6, 9–11, 14–15, 18–20, 23–24, 27–28

November: 1–2, 6–7, 10–11, 15–16, 19–20, 23–25, 28–30

December: 3–5, 8–9, 10–13, 16–17, 21–11, 25–27, 30–31

Special Note: January and March are always the hub or central force from where the spokes of relationships, contacts, communication, and ties start for Cancerians. May and November are the months whirling in the social whirligig. By mixing with people, you multiply your chances of success and happiness. In July, seventy out of 100 times the birth month becomes exceptionally important for luck, changes, relationships. Usually, but not always, it will be one of the most powerful months. September is essential for making contacts, communicating, contracts and tie-ins. The last week of December will be a mighty preparation for reaching out to people and places in 2018.

Secret of Life

Ganesha (whom you may refer to as Allah/Christ/Zoroaster or by any other name) is the ignition key of life's car. To start and launch in the name of Ganesha is to assure success and glory. The power, the dazzling light to see visions, have prophetic dreams, and are all bestowed upon us by Ganesha.

Ganesha says the secret of life is in the ability to change with the changing times. In other words, it is the ability to adapt and adjust to situations, conditions, surroundings, climate change, relationships, and science and technology. His second secret is to keep an open mind. Others are most welcome to their own opinion. The third and final secret is to be true to yourself.

Success Secret of No. 17

Ganesha says the secret of life and astrology is to 'Observe! Observe! Observe!' Angela Merkel of Germany, our own Narendra Modi, former US first lady Michelle Obama, and Muhammad Ali, the world's greatest boxer, were all born on the seventeenth days of their birth months. Here is a picture of the tarot card of number seventeen, called the 'Star'. We can see a lady pouring water on the Earth and providing nourishment. To me the lady is the symbol of the great feminine principle which rules the entire world. There are seven stars in the card. As we all know, seven is the mystical number of spirituality, growth and development.

Narendra Modi, 17 September

Michelle Obama, 17 January

Angela Merkel, 17 July

Muhammad Ali, 17 January

To observe is to see completely and carefully. If you observe the above, you will find that all these four individuals are born on the seventeenth. Secondly, the first alphabet of either the first name or the surname in each case is ‘M’. The tarot card points towards a great and powerful destiny. Therefore, for all these reasons I believe that the number seventeen and the letter ‘M’ go with greatness and glory. Yes, I agree that it may not hold true for all the persons born on the seventeenth of various months. I am open-minded.

Is it but a coincidence or is it fate and destiny? I leave it to you to decide.

World Horoscope 2018

Ganesha says cooking is an art. The challenge lies in the ever-changing nature of the ingredients, the temperature, the flavour, the aroma and the very style of cooking.

The ingredients are: artificial intelligence; healing broken bodies, mind, and spirit (most important); managerial skills of a high order; immense strides in medicine and specially brain power; space travel; robots; biopharmaceuticals; origin of life; God vs technology; climate change; and finally the marriage of technology and humanity.

Let me put it in very simple terms. The years from 2018 to 2020 will have both revolution and evolution. Change is the only constant law of nature. Not only will we survive, we will also prevail. The planets responsible for this constant change in direction are Jupiter, Saturn and Pluto. Jupiter means prosperity, Saturn means inevitable changes and Pluto means drastic and unavoidable situations and effects. These three planets are the trio of the cardinal, ambitious, ruthless sign of duty and responsibility: Capricorn. In short, Capricorn is the father who uses a big stick for others but unhappily not for himself. That is the comedy and the tragedy of the Capricorn sign.

As I have said earlier, this is not the right time for Donald Trump. His world view is one that is corrupted by imagination, illusion and, sometimes, hallucination. The Capricorn North Korean President Kim Jong-un will face terrible times and will be completely defeated in the end by fate. Vladimir Putin of Russia and Theresa May of the UK will find it very difficult to hold on to power. Angela Merkel of Germany is simply wonderful and effective. There is a distinct possibility of a settlement or an understanding between the Jews and the Muslims in 2018 itself. God bless them both. Changes in the regimes in Pakistan and the UK appear certain. In the words of Paul Brenton, 'There is peace behind the tumult, goodness behind the evil, happiness behind the agony.' Nobody has a monopoly over truth, love, justice, mercy, kindness and happiness.

India is certainly tolerant up to a certain extent, but it would be wise, practical and necessary to be much more tolerant and far less rigid and orthodox. Water recycling and the treatment of sewage will be a big changer for our country in 2018 and 2019. It will lead to happiness. I say this in all humility and love for Bharat Mata as I am her child. I certainly bow my head at the feet of Bharat Mata. India comes under the planet of Saturn causing changes that are radical, effective, certain. Our Narendra Modi will hold his own against the world. But India will undergo numerous changes, a few of them could be painful but are necessary in the bigger scheme of events. Not religion but responsibility, duty and development will be the three salient features of India in the coming years.

To be happy we must keep an open mind. Perhaps, I say perhaps the best years will be 2018 and 2021. The year 2021 is most certainly the one when science and technology reign supreme and change the very fabric and direction of all of us. Possibly this is the greatest prediction your humble Ganesha devotee will ever make.

Salute and Tribute

A salute and tribute to the following people:

- Gujarat chief minister Vijay Rupani, in whom I saw a perfect balance in the lines of fate, head and heart on his palms. A great heart and a finely tuned mind.
- Philanthropist and naturalist Firdoz Khambhatta, a dangerously handsome, sharp and brilliant man.
- The lovely Meher Medora, firm of purpose and understanding and sympathetic of heart.

- Aravind Mothi and his sister, Anu Mothi, for offering to make a documentary on my life.
- Hotelier Raj Kumar Jatia for his hospitality and courtesy.
- Behram Mehta for his business acumen fused with immense humility and humanity.
- Jay Shah, son of BJP president Amit Shah, for coming to my house and seeking the blessings of all the mighty spirits and energies of each and every religion.
- The very cultured, civilized, and well-informed education minister of Gujarat, Shri Bhupendra Chudasma for his wisdom as well as his faith in Ganesha.
- Usha Nair, Dr Sunny Shah, Nashit Afroze and their team at the International Human Rights Council for services rendered to NGOs all

over the world. I was very humbled to receive a trophy from them, one I shall always treasure.

- Prince Lakshyaraj of Udaipur for his constant endeavour to help thousands of people through education, NGOs and by example for leading an exemplary life.
- My personal blessings by calling upon all the energies of the world to bless my adopted son Chirag and his fiancée Nikita. They are gems.
- I bow very humbly to my guru, Vashishth Mehta, for coaching me across the path of astrology and spirituality.
- Kudos to Neeraj Bajaj, the son of my late friend and patron Ramkrishna Bajaj, and Dadi Mistry for helping the needy, the weak and the helpless in every possible way. Both are truly magnanimous people.

- Raja Vikram Singh of Jambughoda for his humour and resounding laughter. No wonder his Jambughoda resort is doing immensely well.
- Just as this book is going to press, I met Shiroy and his fiancée, Avasti. Avasti specializes in fashion. Shiroy is an absolute gentleman.
- Lastly, I salute and pay my tribute to all those who seek and serve the cause of peace and goodwill to humanity. To me this is certainly the final word.

About the Author

Born on 11 July 1931, Bejan Daruwalla lives with his wife and their three children. Now, eighty-six years old, he is regarded as one of the hundred greatest astrologers of the last century, as acknowledged by *The Millennium Book of Prophecy* (HarperCollins), having accurately predicted the electoral victory of Narendra Modi at the Kanoria Art Centre, Ahmedabad, on 29 March 2012. Bejan featured on *Hard Talk India* on BBC in August 1999. On 10 December 2010, Bejan was featured in *The Job: Corporate Astrologer* in London's *Financial Times*. Bejan was also awarded the Dr Babasaheb Ambedkar Noble Award on 19 April 2017. Giving Bejan more joy and material achievement was shaking hands with His Holiness the Dalai Lama in December 2013, a moment unforgotten and overwhelming. Bejan has one firm belief: tolerance. He believes everyone has the right to their own ideas and opinions; the perspective of others, even and especially if it differs from one's own, must always be respected.

Important Announcement

Our Ganesha devotee Bejan Daruwalla has moved from Mumbai to Ahmedabad. His Ahmedabad address is:

Bejan Daruwalla

Astrologer and Columnist

C/o Nastur Daruwalla

A-5, Spectrum Towers

Opposite Police Stadium

Shahibag

Ahmedabad 380004

India

Telephone

079-32954387

09825470377

08141234275

Email

info@bejandaruwalla.com

bejandaruwalla@rediffmail.com

Website: www.bejandaruwalla.com